Build Your 1 Billion Content Empire from Scratch

Foundations, Strategies, and Tools to Launch a Content Brand that Attracts and Grows

Dr. Lucas Anderson

Copyright © 2024 by **Lucas Anderson**

All rights reserved. No part of this publication may be reproduced, distributed, or transmitted in any form or by any means, including photocopying, recording, or other electronic or mechanical methods, without the prior written permission of the publisher, except in the case of brief quotations embodied in critical reviews and certain other noncommercial uses permitted by copyright law.

Content creation is a marathon, not a sprint; consistency and quality will always outrun speed.

Content

Content 3

Introduction 7

    The Power of Content in the Digital Age 7

    The Billion-Dollar Opportunity 7

    From Local to Global Reach 8

    The Road Ahead 9

Chapter One 11

    Defining Your Why and Vision 11

    The Bigger Picture 11

    Purpose-Driven Content 12

    Vision Exercise: Practical Steps to Define Your 5-Year Vision 13

Chapter Two 17

    Building Your Content Brand Identity 17

    Brand DNA 17

    Positioning for Success 20

Chapter Three 25

    Audience Mastery: Identifying and Understanding Your Target Audience 25

Deep Audience Research 25

Creating Audience Personas 28

The Power of Engagement 30

Chapter Four 33

Developing a Content Strategy 33

Content Strategy Essentials... 33

Content Planning and Scheduling.................................. 37

Balancing Content Types 39

Chapter Five 43

Crafting Compelling Content.. 43

Content Creation Techniques 43

Storytelling Mastery... 46

Maintaining Quality 49

Chapter Six.. 53

Building Your Content Hub 53

Website and Blog Setup 53

User Experience (UX).. 56

SEO Fundamentals... 58

Chapter Seven 63

Preparing for a Successful Launch 63

Pre-Launch Checklist 63

  Creating Buzz 66

  Launch Day Strategies 69

Chapter Eight 73

  Promoting Your Content 73

  Organic Promotion Strategies 73

  Paid Promotion Basics 77

  Building Partnerships 79

Chapter Nine 83

  Measuring and Analyzing Success 83

  Tracking Key Metrics 83

  Analyzing Data 86

  Refining Your Approach 88

Chapter Ten 91

  Establishing Consistency and Reliability 91

  Content Creation Routines 91

  Maintaining Quality Over Time 94

  Engaging with Your Audience 96

Chapter Eleven 101

  Scaling Your Efforts 101

Outsourcing and Delegation 101

Utilizing Tools and Technology 105

Expanding Your Reach.. 108

Chapter Twelve: 113

Setting the Stage for Future Phases 113

Long-Term Planning 113

Introduction

The Power of Content in the Digital Age

In the vast, ever-evolving landscape of the digital world, content stands as the ultimate catalyst for transformation. It has the power to elevate brands from obscurity to prominence, to turn small startups into global enterprises, and to transform personal passions into billion-dollar ventures. But what makes content such a game-changer in today's world?

The Billion-Dollar Opportunity

Imagine this: a single piece of content has the potential to reach millions, to resonate deeply with audiences, and to drive exponential growth. This isn't a distant dream but a reality that countless individuals and businesses are living right now. Content is no longer just about conveying information; it's about creating meaningful connections and driving impactful interactions.

In the digital age, content serves as the bridge between you and your audience, the conduit through which your message travels across the globe. It's your chance to craft a compelling narrative that captures attention, builds trust, and inspires action. Whether you're a budding entrepreneur, a seasoned business owner, or an aspiring influencer, harnessing the power of content can unlock unparalleled opportunities for growth and success.

Consider the story of an independent fashion designer who started with a modest blog, sharing her designs and inspirations. Through consistent, high-quality content and strategic social media engagement, she built a loyal following. What began as a side project turned into a thriving global brand, with her designs now gracing runways around the world. This is the essence of the billion-dollar opportunity that content presents—transformative potential if wielded with skill and intent.

From Local to Global Reach

Scaling a content brand from local to international isn't just about reaching a broader audience; it's about crafting a strategy that resonates across cultures and borders. The journey from a niche market to a global presence requires a keen understanding of diverse audiences and the ability to adapt your message while maintaining authenticity.

To illustrate, think of a small food blogger who started by sharing recipes tailored to a local palate. As she expanded her content to include international cuisines and collaborated with global food influencers, her blog's reach grew exponentially. By leveraging targeted content strategies and engaging with a wider audience through multiple channels, she transformed her local blog into a global culinary sensation.

Scaling your content empire involves thoughtful planning, strategic partnerships, and an unwavering commitment to delivering value. It's about expanding your vision, adapting your approach, and staying true to your core message while navigating the complexities of a global audience.

The Road Ahead

In this book, we will embark on a comprehensive journey to build your content empire from scratch. We will start by laying a solid foundation—defining your vision, establishing your brand identity, and mastering your target audience. From there, we'll delve into creating and launching compelling content, promoting it effectively, and preparing for future growth.

Each chapter is designed to provide you with actionable insights and practical strategies, ensuring that you not only understand the principles of content creation but also know how to apply them to achieve tangible results. You'll learn how to craft a powerful content strategy, engage with your audience authentically, and scale your efforts to reach new heights.

As you turn these pages, remember that building a content empire is not just about producing content; it's about creating a legacy. It's about making an impact, sharing your story, and connecting with your audience in ways that drive growth and inspire change.

Welcome to the journey of building your 1 billion content empire. The road ahead is filled with opportunities and challenges, but with the right strategies and a relentless passion for your craft, the possibilities are limitless. Let's begin this transformative journey together.

Chapter One

Defining Your Why and Vision

In the realm of content creation, the journey begins long before you hit "publish" on your first post. It starts with understanding why you're creating content in the first place and crafting a vision that will guide every step of your journey. Without a clear vision, your efforts may lack direction and purpose. This chapter is dedicated to helping you define your "why" and establish a compelling vision that will drive your content empire forward.

The Bigger Picture

Think of your vision as the North Star for your content creation journey. It's the guiding light that directs your course, helps you make strategic decisions, and ensures that your content remains aligned with your broader goals. A clear vision not only motivates you but also resonates with your audience, creating a strong foundation for building a loyal following.

Consider the story of Pat Flynn, a successful entrepreneur and podcaster. Pat started his blog, Smart Passive Income, after being laid off from his architecture job. His initial vision was clear: he wanted to create a platform where he could share his journey and help others achieve financial freedom through passive income streams. This vision wasn't just about creating content; it was about making a significant impact on people's lives. His clarity of purpose attracted a dedicated audience and helped him build a successful content empire.

To define your vision, start by asking yourself: What change do I want to see in the world? How can my content contribute to that change? Your vision should be aspirational and deeply connected to your core values and passions.

Purpose-Driven Content

Purpose-driven content is content that goes beyond just informing or entertaining; it's content that inspires, motivates, and creates a meaningful connection with your audience. When your content is driven by a larger mission, it not only engages your audience but also fosters a sense of community and loyalty.

Take the example of **Marie Forleo**, a renowned entrepreneur and author. Her platform, **MarieTV**, is built on the mission to help people create a business and life they love. Marie's content is purpose-driven, focusing on empowering her audience with actionable advice and inspiration. This clear sense of purpose has helped her build a passionate community and establish herself as a trusted authority in her field.

To create purpose-driven content, ask yourself: What values and beliefs are at the heart of my brand? How can my content reflect these values and address the needs and aspirations of my audience? Align your content strategy with your larger mission to create a deeper connection with your audience.

Vision Exercise: Practical Steps to Define Your 5-Year Vision

Defining a 5-year vision for your content empire involves setting clear, actionable goals and envisioning where you want to be in the future. Here are some practical steps to help you craft a compelling vision:

1. **Reflect on Your Passion and Purpose**
    - ❖ Spend some time reflecting on what truly excites you and what you're passionate about. Consider how these passions align with the needs and interests of your target audience.

- Write down your core values and beliefs. How can these be integrated into your content strategy?

2. **Define Your Long-Term Goals**

    - Visualize where you want your content empire to be in 5 years. What milestones do you hope to achieve? This could include audience growth, revenue targets, or impact goals.

    - Set specific, measurable goals. For example, instead of saying, "I want to grow my audience," say, "I want to reach 500,000 subscribers on my YouTube channel."

3. **Create a Vision Statement**

    - Craft a concise and inspiring vision statement that encapsulates your long-term goals and mission. This statement should be a guiding reference for all your content decisions.

    - For example: "To empower aspiring entrepreneurs around the world with actionable strategies and inspirational content that fosters personal and professional growth."

4. **Develop a Roadmap**

   ❖ Break down your 5-year vision into smaller, actionable steps. Create a roadmap that outlines the key initiatives and milestones for each year.

   ❖ Identify the resources, skills, and strategies you need to achieve your goals. This might include content creation tools, marketing strategies, or partnerships.

5. **Revisit and Revise**

   ❖ Regularly revisit your vision and roadmap to ensure they remain aligned with your evolving goals and the changing landscape of your industry.

   ❖ Be open to revising your vision as you gain new insights and experiences. Flexibility is key to adapting and thriving in the dynamic world of content creation.

By following these steps, you'll lay a strong foundation for your content empire, guided by a clear and compelling vision. Your "why" will not only drive your content creation but also resonate deeply with your audience, creating a lasting impact and fostering a dedicated community.

In the following chapters, we'll delve into building your brand identity, mastering your audience, and developing a content strategy that aligns with your vision. But for now, take the time to define your purpose and craft a vision that will serve as your guiding star on this exciting journey.

Chapter Two

Building Your Content Brand Identity

In the crowded digital marketplace, where every second someone is uploading new content, how do you make your voice stand out? Building a distinct content brand identity is crucial for distinguishing yourself and forging a strong connection with your audience. This chapter will guide you through crafting your brand's voice, positioning yourself for success, and harnessing the power of authenticity to create a compelling and memorable content brand.

Brand DNA

Your brand's DNA is its essence—what makes it unique and memorable. It encompasses your brand's voice, tone, and unique value proposition. Getting these elements right will help you connect with your audience on a deeper level and stand out in a sea of content.

1. Crafting Your Brand's Voice

Think of your brand's voice as the personality behind your content. It's how you communicate with your audience and how they perceive you. Your voice should be consistent across all platforms and content types to build a cohesive brand identity.

Example: Consider how Neil Patel, a digital marketing expert, communicates through his blog and videos. His voice is authoritative yet approachable, reflecting his deep expertise while remaining accessible to his audience. This consistency helps build trust and makes his brand instantly recognizable.

Steps to Define Your Brand's Voice:

- ❖ **Identify Your Brand's Personality**: Are you formal or casual, humorous or serious? Define your brand's personality traits.

- ❖ **Choose Your Tone**: Your tone can vary based on the context but should align with your overall personality. For instance, you might be informative in blog posts but more conversational in social media.

- ❖ **Create a Voice Guidelines Document**: Outline specific rules and examples for maintaining consistency in your content.

2. Developing Your Unique Value Proposition (UVP)

Your UVP is what sets you apart from competitors and provides a compelling reason for your audience to choose your content over others. It's the core benefit or solution you offer that meets your audience's needs.

Example: Marie Forleo's UVP is to provide actionable advice that empowers entrepreneurs to build businesses and lives they love. Her content focuses on practical strategies and motivational insights, differentiating her from others who might offer less actionable content.

Steps to Define Your UVP:

- **Analyze Your Competitors**: Identify gaps in the market and areas where you can provide unique value.
- **Understand Your Audience's Needs**: Conduct research to find out what your audience is looking for and how you can address those needs.
- **Craft Your UVP Statement**: Write a clear, concise statement that communicates the unique benefit you offer.

Positioning for Success

Once you've established your brand's DNA, the next step is positioning yourself effectively in a crowded marketplace. This involves defining your niche, differentiating yourself from competitors, and creating a strong, recognizable brand presence.

1. Finding Your Niche

A niche is a specialized segment of the market for your content. Finding and focusing on your niche allows you to target a specific audience more effectively and build a loyal following.

Example: Tim Ferriss found his niche in productivity and personal optimization. By focusing on this specific area and sharing his experiences and insights, he built a highly engaged audience interested in maximizing their efficiency and achieving their goals.

Steps to Identify Your Niche:

- ❖ **Assess Your Interests and Expertise**: Determine what topics you are passionate about and where your expertise lies.

- **Research Market Demand**: Use tools like Google Trends and social media insights to gauge interest in your chosen niche.

- **Define Your Target Audience**: Create detailed audience personas to understand their needs and preferences.

2. Differentiating Yourself

To stand out, you need to offer something different from what's already available. This could be a unique perspective, innovative content formats, or exceptional value.

Example: Gordon Ramsay differentiated himself in the culinary world by combining his high culinary standards with a fiery personality on television. His unique approach to cooking shows set him apart from other chefs and created a strong personal brand.

Steps to Differentiate Yourself:

- **Analyze Competitors**: Identify what others in your niche are doing and find ways to offer something unique.

- **Leverage Your Strengths**: Highlight what makes you different, whether it's your unique perspective, skills, or experiences.

- **Innovate Continuously**: Stay ahead of trends and continually refine your approach to maintain a fresh and distinct brand.

The Power of Authenticity

Authenticity is the cornerstone of building trust and credibility with your audience. Your personal or brand story can significantly enhance your content's impact and foster a deeper connection with your audience.

1. Leveraging Your Story

Your story, whether it's your personal journey, your brand's origin, or your mission, can resonate powerfully with your audience. Sharing your story creates an emotional connection and helps humanize your brand.

Example: Humans of New York, created by Brandon Stanton, leverages real-life stories of people from New York City. Each story is authentic and personal, creating a deep emotional bond with readers and making the content highly relatable and engaging.

Steps to Share Your Story:

- ❖ **Identify Key Elements of Your Story**: What are the pivotal moments or experiences that have shaped your journey?
- ❖ **Be Honest and Transparent**: Share your story openly, including challenges and successes.
- ❖ **Connect Your Story to Your Content**: Relate your personal experiences to the value you provide through your content.

2. Building Trust Through Consistency

Consistency in your messaging and content delivery reinforces your authenticity and helps build trust with your audience. When your audience knows what to expect from you, they are more likely to engage and remain loyal.

Example: Pat Flynn's consistency in providing valuable, actionable content has built a high level of trust with his audience. His transparent approach to sharing his business strategies and results has solidified his credibility and loyalty among followers.

Steps to Ensure Consistency:

- **Develop a Content Calendar**: Plan and schedule your content to maintain a regular posting rhythm.

- **Maintain a Consistent Tone and Voice**: Ensure that your brand's voice and tone remain uniform across all platforms and content types.

- **Engage Regularly with Your Audience**: Respond to comments and feedback consistently to build and maintain trust.

In summary, building a strong content brand identity involves defining your brand's voice, creating a unique value proposition, positioning yourself effectively, and leveraging authenticity. By following these steps and learning from real-life examples, you'll create a compelling and memorable content brand that stands out and resonates with your audience.

Chapter Three

Audience Mastery: Identifying and Understanding Your Target Audience

To build a successful content empire, it's crucial to know who you're creating for. Understanding your target audience is not just about demographics; it's about delving into their needs, desires, and behaviors. This chapter will explore methods for deep audience research, the creation of detailed audience personas, and strategies for engaging and nurturing a loyal community.

Deep Audience Research

Knowing your audience is the bedrock of effective content creation. Deep audience research involves more than just gathering basic demographic information. It's about uncovering what drives your audience, what challenges they face, and what kind of content resonates with them.

1. Conducting Surveys and Interviews

One of the most direct ways to understand your audience is to ask them. Surveys and interviews provide valuable insights into their preferences, pain points, and expectations.

Example: Buffer, a popular social media management tool, uses surveys to gather feedback from their users. By regularly conducting surveys, they can understand their users' needs and refine their product offerings accordingly. For instance, feedback from users led to the development of new features that addressed specific user needs.

Steps to Conduct Surveys and Interviews:

- **Design Your Questions**: Focus on open-ended questions that elicit detailed responses about challenges, preferences, and content types.

- **Use Online Tools**: Platforms like SurveyMonkey or Google Forms make it easy to distribute surveys and collect responses.

- **Analyze the Data**: Look for patterns and trends in the responses to identify common needs and desires.

2. Analyzing Analytics and Social Media Insights

Digital analytics tools and social media platforms provide a wealth of information about your audience's behavior and engagement with your content.

Example: HubSpot, a leading marketing platform, utilizes analytics to track how visitors interact with their content. By analyzing metrics such as time on page, bounce rate, and social media shares, they gain insights into what types of content are most effective and adjust their strategy accordingly.

Steps to Use Analytics and Insights:

- **Monitor Engagement Metrics**: Track metrics such as page views, click-through rates, and social media engagement to understand what resonates with your audience.

- **Segment Your Audience**: Use analytics to identify different audience segments and tailor content to each group's preferences.

- **Adapt Your Strategy**: Use insights to refine your content strategy and focus on topics that generate the most interest.

3. Competitor Analysis

Understanding what your competitors are doing can provide valuable insights into your audience's preferences and gaps in the market.

Example: A food blogger analyzing competitors' content might notice a gap in vegan recipe content. By filling this niche, they can attract a specific audience segment interested in vegan cooking.

Steps for Competitor Analysis:

- ❖ **Identify Key Competitors**: Research competitors who target a similar audience.
- ❖ **Evaluate Their Content**: Analyze their content types, engagement levels, and audience feedback.
- ❖ **Find Gaps and Opportunities**: Identify areas where competitors may be lacking and explore opportunities to address these gaps.

Creating Audience Personas

Audience personas are fictional, generalized representations of your ideal audience segments. They help you tailor your content to meet the specific needs and preferences of different groups.

1. Gathering Information for Personas

Creating detailed personas involves gathering and synthesizing information from various sources.

Example: The digital marketing agency Neil Patel Digital uses detailed personas to tailor their marketing strategies. By segmenting their audience into personas such as "Small Business Owners" and "Enterprise Marketers," they can create targeted content that addresses each group's unique challenges and goals.

Steps to Create Audience Personas:

- **Compile Demographic Data**: Gather information such as age, gender, location, and occupation.
- **Include Psychographic Details**: Identify interests, values, and lifestyle choices.
- **Create Persona Profiles**: Develop detailed profiles that include goals, challenges, and content preferences.

2. Using Personas to Guide Content Creation

Once you have developed your personas, use them to guide your content creation process.

Example: A tech company might create separate content streams for their "Tech Enthusiast" persona and their "IT Manager" persona, focusing on the latest gadgets for the former and industry insights for the latter.

Steps to Use Personas Effectively:

- ❖ **Tailor Content to Each Persona**: Create content that speaks directly to the needs and interests of each persona.

- ❖ **Adjust Your Tone and Messaging**: Customize your tone and messaging to resonate with different personas.

- ❖ **Evaluate and Refine**: Regularly review and update your personas based on feedback and changing trends.

The Power of Engagement

Engagement is the process of building and nurturing relationships with your audience. It involves interacting with them, responding to their feedback, and creating a sense of community.

1. Building a community

Creating a sense of community around your content fosters loyalty and encourages active participation.

Example: Pat Flynn's Smart Passive Income community is a prime example of successful engagement. Through forums, webinars, and social media groups, Pat has built a vibrant community where members support each other and share their experiences.

Steps to Build a community:

- **Create Engaging Content**: Develop content that encourages interaction, such as Q&A sessions, polls, and discussion topics.
- **Foster Interaction**: Actively engage with your audience by responding to comments and participating in discussions.
- **Encourage User-Generated Content**: Invite your audience to contribute content, such as guest posts or testimonials.

2. Nurturing Relationships

Maintaining ongoing engagement with your audience helps build trust and loyalty.

Example: Email marketing campaigns are a powerful tool for nurturing relationships. Companies like KISS metrics send personalized emails based on user behavior, providing relevant content and updates that keep their audience engaged.

Steps to Nurture Relationships:

- ❖ **Develop an Email Strategy**: Use email newsletters to provide value and stay connected with your audience.

- ❖ **Personalize Your Communication**: Tailor your messages based on audience preferences and behaviors.

- ❖ **Solicit Feedback**: Regularly ask for feedback to understand how you can better serve your audience.

Mastering your audience involves deep research to understand their needs and preferences, creating detailed personas to guide your content strategy, and actively engaging with your community.

Chapter Four

Developing a Content Strategy

Creating a robust content strategy is essential for building a successful content empire. A well-crafted strategy provides direction, ensures consistency, and helps you achieve your goals. This chapter will delve into the essentials of developing a comprehensive content plan, best practices for planning and scheduling content, and the benefits of balancing different content types.

Content Strategy Essentials

A content strategy is a roadmap that outlines how you will create, publish, and manage your content to achieve specific business goals. It's more than just a collection of ideas; it's a strategic approach to delivering value to your audience.

1. Define Your Objectives

Your content strategy should start with clear objectives. What do you want to achieve with your content? Objectives might include increasing brand awareness, generating leads, or driving website traffic.

Example: Red Bull's content strategy focuses on building brand awareness and engagement through extreme sports and adventure content. Their objective is to position Red Bull as more than just a beverage, but a lifestyle brand associated with excitement and energy.

Steps to Define Objectives:

- **Set SMART Goals**: Ensure your objectives are Specific, Measurable, Achievable, Relevant, and Time-bound.

- **Align with Business Goals**: Make sure your content objectives support your overall business goals.

- **Measure Success**: Determine how you will measure the success of your content efforts (e.g., through KPIs like website traffic or conversion rates).

2. Understand Your Audience

Your content should be tailored to your target audience's needs and preferences. Deep audience research, as discussed in Chapter 3, is crucial for understanding what type of content will resonate with them.

Steps to Understand Your Audience:

- **Develop Audience Personas**: Use detailed profiles to guide your content creation (see Chapter 3 for more on this).

- **Analyze Audience Insights**: Leverage analytics tools to understand content performance and audience engagement.

- **Gather Feedback**: Regularly solicit feedback from your audience to refine your content strategy.

3. Craft Your Key Messages

Identify the core messages you want to communicate through your content. These should reflect your brand's values and resonate with your audience's interests and needs.

Example: Apple's content strategy emphasizes innovation, design, and simplicity. Their key messages are communicated through sleek product presentations and inspirational marketing campaigns, reinforcing their brand identity.

Steps to Craft Key Messages:

- **Identify Core Themes**: Determine the main themes or topics that align with your brand's values and audience interests.

- **Develop Messaging Guidelines**: Create guidelines for how these messages should be communicated across different content types.

- **Ensure Consistency**: Maintain consistency in messaging across all content to reinforce your brand identity.

4. Plan Your Content Formats

Different content formats can achieve different goals. Consider how various formats can be used to engage your audience and deliver your key messages.

Steps to Plan Content Formats:

- **Identify Effective Formats**: Based on your audience research, determine which content formats (e.g., blog posts, videos, infographics) are most effective.

- **Develop a Content Mix**: Plan a diverse content mix that includes various formats to keep your audience engaged.

- **Align Formats with Objectives**: Ensure that the formats you choose align with your content objectives (e.g., videos for brand awareness, case studies for lead generation).

Content Planning and Scheduling

A well-organized content calendar helps ensure consistency and keeps your content efforts on track. It's a tool for planning what content will be published, when, and on which platforms.

1. Developing a Content Calendar

A content calendar is a detailed schedule that outlines when and where content will be published. It helps you plan ahead, manage resources, and maintain a consistent posting rhythm.

Example: HubSpot uses a content calendar to plan and coordinate their blog posts, social media updates, and email newsletters. This systematic approach ensures that they publish content consistently and align it with marketing campaigns.

Steps to Develop a Content Calendar:

- **Choose a Planning Tool**: Use tools like Google Calendar, Trello, or dedicated content calendar software.

- **Plan Content Topics**: Outline content topics and themes for each month or week based on your strategy.

- **Schedule Publishing Dates**: Set specific dates and times for publishing content.

- **Assign Responsibilities**: Designate team members responsible for creating and publishing content.

2. Best Practices for Scheduling

Effective scheduling ensures that content is published consistently and aligns with your overall strategy.

Steps for Effective Scheduling:

- **Consider Peak Times**: Schedule content to be published during times when your audience is most active.

- **Plan for Flexibility**: Allow room for adjustments based on current events, trends, or audience feedback.

- **Balance Frequency**: Determine the optimal frequency for publishing content to avoid overwhelming your audience or stretching your resources.

3. Monitor and Adjust

Regularly review your content calendar and adjust as needed based on performance data and feedback.

Steps to Monitor and Adjust:

- **Track Performance Metrics**: Use analytics tools to measure the effectiveness of your content.
- **Solicit Feedback**: Gather feedback from your audience to understand their preferences and needs.
- **Make Adjustments**: Update your content calendar based on performance insights and audience feedback.

Balancing Content Types

A diverse content mix keeps your audience engaged and caters to different preferences and needs. Balancing various content types can enhance your content strategy and drive better results.

1. Exploring Content Formats

Different formats serve different purposes and appeal to different segments of your audience.

Example: Moz, a leading SEO software company, uses a mix of blog posts, webinars, and guides to engage their audience. Blog posts provide quick tips and insights, webinars offer in-depth learning opportunities, and guides serve as comprehensive resources.

Steps to Explore Content Formats:

- ❖ **Identify Key Formats**: Determine which formats (e.g., blog posts, videos, infographics, podcasts) are most suitable for your audience and objectives.

- ❖ **Evaluate Benefits**: Understand the benefits of each format, such as video for visual storytelling or infographics for complex data.

- ❖ **Experiment and Adapt**: Try different formats and analyze their performance to find what works best for your audience.

2. Integrating Different Content Types

A balanced content strategy integrates various content types to provide value and maintain audience interest.

Steps to Integrate Content Types:

- **Create a Content Mix**: Plan a diverse content mix that includes different formats and types.
- **Align with Objectives**: Ensure that each content type aligns with your strategic objectives and contributes to your overall goals.
- **Maintain Consistency**: Keep your brand's voice and messaging consistent across all content types.

3. Measuring Effectiveness

Evaluate the performance of different content types to understand what resonates with your audience.

Steps to Measure Effectiveness:

- **Track Performance Metrics**: Measure engagement, reach, and conversion rates for each content type.
- **Analyze Audience Feedback**: Review comments, shares, and other feedback to gauge audience response.
- **Refine Your Strategy**: Use insights to refine your content strategy and focus on formats that drive the best results.

In summary, developing a content strategy involves defining clear objectives, understanding your audience, crafting key messages, planning content formats, and maintaining an organized content calendar. By balancing different content types and measuring effectiveness, you'll create a comprehensive strategy that drives engagement, achieves your goals, and supports the growth of your content empire.

Chapter Five

Crafting Compelling Content

Crafting compelling content is at the heart of building a successful content empire. High-quality content not only attracts but also retains your audience. This chapter will explore best practices for content creation, the art of storytelling, and strategies for maintaining quality standards.

Content Creation Techniques

Creating content that stands out requires more than just writing skills. It involves understanding your audience, delivering value, and employing techniques that make your content engaging and impactful.

1. Understanding Your Audience's Needs

Before you create content, you need to know what your audience wants. This requires a deep understanding of their pain points, interests, and preferences.

Example: HubSpot's blog is known for its high-quality, valuable content because they meticulously research their audience's needs. By analyzing search queries, social media discussions, and industry trends, they tailor their content to address specific challenges faced by their readers.

Steps to Understand Audience Needs:

- **Conduct Audience Research**: Use surveys, interviews, and analytics to gather insights.
- **Identify Pain Points**: Determine the common problems or questions your audience has.
- **Deliver Solutions**: Create content that addresses these needs and offers practical solutions.

2. Creating Engaging Headlines

Your headline is the first thing readers see, so it needs to grab their attention and make them want to read more.

Example: Neil Patel's blog headlines often include actionable advice or intriguing questions, such as "How to Increase Your Website Traffic by 200% in 30 Days." This approach piques curiosity and promises value.

Steps to Craft Effective Headlines:

- **Be Specific and Clear**: Clearly convey what the content will deliver.

- **Use Power Words**: Incorporate compelling words that evoke emotion or curiosity.
- **Test and Refine**: Experiment with different headlines and analyze their performance.

3. Writing High-Quality Content

High-quality content is well-researched, informative, and engaging. It provides value to the reader and is easy to understand.

Steps to Write High-Quality Content:

- **Research Thoroughly**: Base your content on accurate, up-to-date information.
- **Use Clear and Concise Language**: Avoid jargon and make your content accessible.
- **Incorporate Visuals**: Use images, infographics, and videos to enhance understanding and engagement.

4. Optimizing for SEO

Search engine optimization (SEO) helps your content reach a wider audience by improving its visibility in search engine results.

Example: Moz's blog incorporates SEO best practices, such as using relevant keywords, optimizing meta descriptions, and creating internal links. This helps their content rank higher in search results and attract more readers.

Steps for SEO Optimization:

- **Conduct Keyword Research**: Identify relevant keywords and phrases.
- **Optimize On-Page Elements**: Include keywords in titles, headers, and meta descriptions.
- **Build Backlinks**: Encourage other reputable sites to link to your content.

Storytelling Mastery

Storytelling is a powerful tool for creating compelling content. Stories resonate with people on an emotional level and make your content more memorable and engaging.

1. Crafting a Strong Narrative

A well-crafted story has a clear structure: a beginning, middle, and end. It captures attention, builds interest, and concludes with a satisfying resolution.

Example: Airbnb's marketing campaign often features stories from hosts and guests. These personal narratives highlight unique experiences and create an emotional connection with the audience, making their brand more relatable and memorable.

Steps to Craft a Strong Narrative:

- **Start with a Hook**: Grab the reader's attention with an intriguing opening.

- **Develop Characters**: Introduce relatable characters who face challenges or conflicts.

- **Include a Resolution**: Provide a satisfying conclusion that ties everything together.

2. Using Emotional Triggers

Emotional triggers can significantly enhance the impact of your content. By evoking emotions such as joy, sadness, or surprise, you can create a stronger connection with your audience.

Example: Dove's "Real Beauty" campaign uses emotional storytelling to challenge traditional beauty standards and promote self-esteem. Their content resonates deeply with audiences by addressing real-life issues and celebrating diversity.

Steps to Use Emotional Triggers:

- **Identify Key Emotions**: Determine which emotions you want to evoke in your audience.

- **Incorporate Emotional Elements**: Use language, visuals, and stories that evoke these emotions.

- **Be Authentic**: Ensure that the emotions you evoke align with your brand's values and message.

3. Creating Relatable Characters

Characters in your stories should be relatable and reflect the experiences of your audience. This helps build a connection and makes your content more engaging.

Example: Case studies often feature relatable characters such as small business owners or everyday users. By showcasing their successes and challenges, these stories help readers see how the content applies to their own lives.

Steps to Create Relatable Characters:

- **Understand Your Audience**: Develop characters that reflect your audience's demographics and experiences.

- **Highlight Common Challenges**: Focus on challenges or situations that your audience can relate to.

- **Show Growth and Success**: Illustrate how the characters overcome obstacles and achieve their goals.

Maintaining Quality

Ensuring high standards in content production is essential for building trust and credibility with your audience. Quality content reflects well on your brand and keeps readers coming back.

1. Establishing Content Standards

Set clear guidelines for content creation to maintain consistency and quality.

Example: The New York Times has a rigorous editorial process that includes fact-checking, editing, and adherence to journalistic standards. This ensures that all content meets high-quality standards before publication.

Steps to Establish Content Standards:

- **Create Guidelines**: Develop guidelines for tone, style, and formatting.

- **Implement a Review Process**: Set up a process for reviewing and editing content before publication.
- **Provide Training**: Train your content creators on best practices and standards.

2. Editing and Proofreading

Editing and proofreading are crucial for ensuring that your content is free from errors and polished.

Steps for Effective Editing and Proofreading:

- **Review for Clarity**: Check for clarity, coherence, and readability.
- **Correct Grammar and Spelling**: Ensure that the content is free from grammatical and spelling errors.
- **Use Editing Tools**: Leverage tools like Grammarly or Hemingway to assist in the editing process.

3. Continuous Improvement

Regularly review and update your content to keep it relevant and high-quality.

Steps for Continuous Improvement:

- ❖ **Monitor Performance**: Track how your content performs and gather feedback from readers.

- ❖ **Update Content**: Refresh outdated content and add new information as needed.

- ❖ **Learn and Adapt**: Stay updated on industry trends and best practices to continuously improve your content strategy.

Crafting compelling content involves understanding your audience's needs, creating engaging headlines, writing high-quality content, optimizing for SEO, mastering storytelling, and maintaining high standards. By following these practices and continuously refining your approach, you'll produce content that captivates your audience and drives the success of your content empire.

Focus on producing valuable and consistent content over time instead of rushing to produce content quickly with short-term results in mind

Chapter Six

Building Your Content Hub

A content hub is the central platform where your audience engages with your content. It's essential for establishing your online presence, building a loyal audience, and driving your content strategy. This chapter will guide you through setting up an effective content hub, designing a user-friendly experience, and implementing SEO fundamentals to enhance visibility.

Website and Blog Setup

Your website and blog are the cornerstone of your content hub. They serve as the primary destination for your audience to access your content and engage with your brand.

1. Choosing a Domain Name and Hosting

Your domain name should be memorable, relevant, and reflective of your brand. Reliable hosting is crucial for ensuring your site is accessible and performs well.

Example: Pat Flynn of Smart Passive Income chose a straightforward domain name that reflects his brand's focus on passive income strategies. Reliable hosting ensures that his site remains accessible and performs well even during high traffic periods.

Steps to Choose a Domain Name and Hosting:

- ❖ **Select a Relevant Domain**: Choose a domain name that is easy to remember and relevant to your brand.

- ❖ **Opt for Reliable Hosting**: Choose a hosting provider with a track record of reliability and good customer support.

- ❖ **Consider Scalability**: Ensure that your hosting plan can accommodate your growing needs.

2. Designing Your Website

Your website design should reflect your brand's identity and provide a seamless experience for users.

Example: Squarespace is known for its sleek and user-friendly templates. Many content creators use Squarespace to build visually appealing websites that are easy to navigate and align with their brand aesthetics.

Steps to Design Your Website:

- ❖ **Choose a Platform**: Select a website building platform (e.g., WordPress, Squarespace, Wix) based on your needs and technical skills.

- **Select a Template**: Choose a template that aligns with your brand's style and customize it to fit your needs.

- **Design for Usability**: Ensure that your website is easy to navigate and visually appealing.

3. Setting Up Your Blog

A blog is a key component of your content hub, allowing you to regularly publish and share content with your audience.

Steps to Set Up Your Blog:

- **Create a Blog Page**: Set up a dedicated blog page on your website where all your posts will be displayed.

- **Organize Categories and Tags**: Use categories and tags to organize your content and make it easier for readers to find relevant posts.

- **Enable Comments**: Allow readers to comment on your posts to encourage engagement and feedback.

User Experience (UX)

Designing for a positive user experience is crucial for keeping your audience engaged and ensuring they can easily access and interact with your content.

1. Designing for Accessibility

Ensure that your website is accessible to all users, including those with disabilities.

Example: The American Foundation for the Blind's website is designed with accessibility in mind, including features like text-to-speech and high-contrast modes to support users with visual impairments.

Steps to Design for Accessibility:

- ❖ **Use Alt Text**: Provide descriptive alt text for images to assist screen readers.

- ❖ **Ensure Keyboard Navigation**: Make sure users can navigate your site using only a keyboard.

- ❖ **Offer Text Alternatives**: Provide text alternatives for multimedia content, such as transcripts for videos.

2. Enhancing Site Navigation

Easy navigation is essential for a positive user experience. Users should be able to find what they're looking for quickly and effortlessly.

Example: Amazon's website features a highly intuitive navigation system with clear categories, filters, and a powerful search function, making it easy for users to find and purchase products.

Steps to Enhance Site Navigation:

- **Create a Clear Menu**: Design a menu that includes key sections and is easy to access.
- **Implement Search Functionality**: Include a search bar to help users find specific content.
- **Use Breadcrumbs**: Implement breadcrumbs to help users understand their location on the site.

3. Improving Page Load Speed

Fast-loading pages enhance user experience and reduce bounce rates.

Example: Google's Page Speed Insights tool helps website owners analyze and improve their page load speeds, ensuring a smooth and fast experience for users.

Steps to Improve Page Load Speed:

- ❖ **Optimize Images**: Compress images to reduce their file size.

- ❖ **Minimize HTTP Requests**: Reduce the number of elements on your page that require HTTP requests.

- ❖ **Leverage Browser Caching**: Use browser caching to store static resources and improve load times for returning visitors.

SEO Fundamentals

Search engine optimization (SEO) is essential for improving your content's visibility and attracting organic traffic to your content hub.

1. Keyword Research

Identifying the right keywords helps you understand what your audience is searching for and enables you to create content that meets their needs.

Example: Ahrefs provides keyword research tools that help users identify high-traffic keywords and analyze competitors' strategies, allowing them to optimize their content effectively.

Steps for Keyword Research:

- **Use Keyword Tools**: Utilize tools like Google Keyword Planner or Ahrefs to find relevant keywords.

- **Analyze Search Intent**: Understand the intent behind the keywords to create content that addresses users' needs.

- **Incorporate Keywords Strategically**: Include keywords in titles, headings, and throughout your content.

2. On-Page SEO

On-page SEO involves optimizing individual pages to rank higher in search results.

Example: Backlink's blog posts are optimized with relevant keywords, engaging meta descriptions, and well-structured headings, contributing to their high search engine rankings.

Steps for On-Page SEO:

- **Optimize Titles and Meta Descriptions**: Create compelling titles and meta descriptions that include relevant keywords.

- **Use Header Tags**: Organize your content with header tags (H1, H2, H3) to improve readability and SEO.

- **Create Quality Content**: Focus on creating valuable, in-depth content that addresses user queries.

3. Building Backlinks

Backlinks from reputable sites signal to search engines that your content is valuable and authoritative.

Example: Moz's link-building strategies involve creating high-quality content that attracts links from other authoritative sites, enhancing their search engine visibility.

Steps for Building Backlinks:

- **Create Shareable Content**: Develop content that others will want to link to and share.

- **Reach Out to Influencers**: Collaborate with influencers and industry experts to earn backlinks.

- **Monitor Your Backlinks**: Use tools like Ahrefs to track your backlinks and identify opportunities for improvement.

4. Monitoring and Analyzing SEO Performance

Regularly monitoring your SEO performance helps you understand what's working and where improvements are needed.

Steps for Monitoring SEO Performance:

- ❖ **Use Analytics Tools**: Utilize tools like Google Analytics and Google Search Console to track your SEO performance.

- ❖ **Analyze Traffic Sources**: Review where your traffic is coming from and which keywords are driving visitors.

- ❖ **Adjust Your Strategy**: Make data-driven adjustments to your SEO strategy based on performance insights.

Building an effective content hub involves setting up a well-designed website and blog, ensuring a positive user experience, and implementing SEO fundamentals to enhance visibility. By focusing on these areas, you'll create a platform that attracts and engages your audience, supports your content strategy, and drives growth.

Growth isn't measured by numbers alone, but by the depth of engagement and the strength of your brand's impact.

Chapter Seven

Preparing for a Successful Launch

Launching your content hub is a critical moment that sets the stage for your content empire's success. Proper preparation ensures a smooth launch and maximizes its impact. This chapter will guide you through essential pre-launch steps, techniques for generating buzz, and strategies to make the most of launch day.

Pre-Launch Checklist

Before you go live, there are several key steps to ensure everything is in place for a successful launch.

1. Finalize Content and Design

Ensure that all content is polished and your website design is finalized.

Steps to Finalize Content and Design:

- ❖ **Review Content**: Double-check that all articles, blog posts, and multimedia content are proofread, edited, and optimized for SEO.

- **Test Design Elements**: Verify that all design elements are working correctly, including links, images, and navigation.

- **Ensure Mobile Compatibility**: Test your website on various devices to ensure it is mobile-friendly and performs well on different screen sizes.

2. Set Up Analytics and Tracking

Implementing analytics tools allows you to track your launch's performance and gather valuable insights.

Steps to Set Up Analytics and Tracking:

- **Install Google Analytics**: Set up Google Analytics to track visitor behavior, traffic sources, and other key metrics.

- **Configure Google Search Console**: Add your site to Google Search Console to monitor indexing status and identify potential issues.

- **Set Up Conversion Tracking**: Use conversion tracking tools to measure key actions such as sign-ups, downloads, or purchases.

3. Prepare Your Launch Materials

Create all necessary materials for your launch, including press releases, social media posts, and email campaigns.

Steps to Prepare Launch Materials:

- ❖ **Draft Press Releases**: Write a compelling press release announcing your launch and its unique features.

- ❖ **Create Social Media Content**: Develop a series of social media posts to generate excitement and share updates.

- ❖ **Design Email Campaigns**: Craft email campaigns to inform your subscribers about the launch and encourage them to visit your site.

4. Conduct a Final Review

Perform a thorough review to ensure everything is ready for launch.

Steps for a Final Review:

- ❖ **Test Functionality**: Check that all website features, forms, and interactive elements are working as intended.

- **Verify Content Accuracy**: Ensure that all content is accurate and up-to-date.

- **Check Load Times**: Test your website's load times to ensure it performs well under expected traffic levels.

Creating Buzz

Generating excitement and anticipation before your launch can significantly impact its success.

1. Build a Pre-Launch Email List

Gather a list of potential subscribers or interested parties who can be the first to know about your launch.

Steps to Build a Pre-Launch Email List:

- **Offer Incentives**: Provide incentives such as exclusive content, early access, or discounts to encourage sign-ups.

- **Promote Sign-Up Forms**: Use your existing channels, such as social media and your website, to promote your email sign-up forms.

- **Engage with Subscribers**: Send regular updates and teasers to keep your audience engaged and excited about the launch.

2. Leverage social media

Social media is a powerful tool for generating buzz and reaching a wide audience.

Steps to Leverage social media:

- ❖ **Create a Countdown**: Use countdown posts or stories to build anticipation leading up to the launch date.

- ❖ **Engage with Influencers**: Collaborate with influencers or industry experts to amplify your message and reach a larger audience.

- ❖ **Host Giveaways or Contests**: Run contests or giveaways to encourage sharing and increase visibility.

3. Utilize Press and Media

Getting press coverage can significantly boost your launch's visibility.

Steps to Utilize Press and Media:

- ❖ **Pitch to Journalists**: Reach out to journalists and bloggers who cover your industry with a well-crafted pitch.

- **Offer Exclusive Previews**: Provide select media outlets with early access to your content or a sneak peek of your launch.

- **Submit to Industry Publications**: Submit press releases or articles to industry-specific publications and websites.

4. Engage with Your Community

Engaging with your community can create a loyal base of supporters who are excited to share your launch.

Steps to Engage with Your Community:

- **Host Virtual Events**: Organize webinars, live Q&A sessions, or virtual launch parties to interact with your audience.

- **Share Behind-the-Scenes Content**: Provide behind-the-scenes glimpses of your launch preparation to build interest and excitement.

- **Encourage User-Generated Content**: Invite your audience to share their own content related to your launch and feature it on your platforms.

Launch Day Strategies

Maximizing the impact of launch day requires careful planning and execution.

1. Execute Your Launch Plan

Follow through with your planned launch activities to ensure a smooth execution.

Steps to Execute Your Launch Plan:

- ❖ **Go Live on Schedule**: Ensure that your website and all associated content go live at the scheduled time.

- ❖ **Monitor Performance**: Keep an eye on site performance, traffic, and user engagement to address any issues promptly.

- ❖ **Engage with Your Audience**: Be active on social media and respond to comments or inquiries to maintain momentum.

2. Analyze and Adjust

Gather data and insights from your launch day to assess performance and make necessary adjustments.

Steps to Analyze and Adjust:

- **Review Analytics**: Analyze data from Google Analytics and other tracking tools to evaluate traffic, user behavior, and conversion rates.

- **Gather Feedback**: Collect feedback from users and stakeholders to identify areas for improvement.

- **Make Immediate Changes**: Address any issues or feedback promptly to enhance user experience and performance.

3. Celebrate and Reflect

Take time to celebrate your launch and reflect on the process to learn from your experience.

Steps to Celebrate and Reflect:

- **Acknowledge Your Team**: Recognize the efforts of your team and collaborators who contributed to the launch.

- **Reflect on Learnings**: Evaluate what worked well and what could be improved for future launches.

- **Share Your Success**: Publicly share the success of your launch with your audience and express gratitude for their support.

Preparing for a successful launch involves thorough planning, generating buzz, and executing strategies effectively on launch day. By following these steps, you'll set the stage for a successful launch that captures attention, drives engagement, and lays a strong foundation for the growth of your content empire.

Content without purpose is noise, but content with vision creates legacies.

Chapter Eight

Promoting Your Content

Promotion is key to ensuring your content reaches its intended audience and achieves its desired impact. This chapter delves into effective organic and paid promotion strategies and explores the benefits of building partnerships to expand your content's reach.

Organic Promotion Strategies

Organic promotion involves leveraging free methods to drive traffic and engagement to your content. It includes utilizing social media, SEO, and email marketing to attract and retain your audience.

1. Leveraging social media

Social media platforms are powerful tools for promoting content and engaging with your audience.

Steps to Leverage social media:

- ❖ **Choose the Right Platforms**: Focus on platforms where your target audience is most active. For instance, Instagram and TikTok are great for visual content, while LinkedIn is ideal for professional and B2B content.

Example: Buffer's social media strategy includes a strong presence on Twitter and LinkedIn, where they share valuable insights and engage with their audience.

- ❖ **Create Shareable Content**: Develop content that resonates with your audience and encourages sharing. Use engaging visuals, compelling headlines, and interactive elements.

Example: BuzzFeed's viral content often includes quizzes, listicles, and videos designed to be highly shareable and engaging.

- ❖ **Engage with Your Audience**: Respond to comments, participate in discussions, and encourage user-generated content to build a community around your brand.

Example: Wendy's Twitter account is known for its witty and engaging responses to followers, creating a strong and interactive community.

2. SEO (Search Engine Optimization)

SEO is crucial for improving your content's visibility in search engine results, driving organic traffic to your site.

Steps to Optimize for SEO:

- **Conduct Keyword Research**: Identify relevant keywords that your audience is searching for and incorporate them into your content.

Example: Neil Patel's blog uses thorough keyword research to create content optimized for high-traffic keywords, helping his site rank well in search results.

- **Optimize On-Page Elements**: Ensure that titles, meta descriptions, headers, and content include targeted keywords and are structured for readability and SEO.

Example: HubSpot's blog posts are meticulously optimized with keywords, meta descriptions, and engaging headlines to rank well in search results.

- **Build Quality Backlinks**: Earn backlinks from reputable sites to boost your content's authority and search engine ranking.

Example: Moz's link-building strategies include creating valuable content that naturally attracts backlinks from other authoritative websites.

3. Email Marketing

Email marketing allows you to directly reach your audience and drive traffic to your content.

Steps to Utilize Email Marketing:

- ❖ **Build an Email List**: Collect email addresses through sign-up forms on your website, social media, and other channels.

Example: ConvertKit uses lead magnets, such as free eBooks and webinars, to grow its email list and nurture subscribers.

- ❖ **Create Engaging Newsletters**: Design newsletters that provide value, such as exclusive content, updates, and personalized recommendations.

Example: TheSkimm's daily newsletter is known for its concise and engaging summaries of news, keeping subscribers informed and engaged.

- ❖ **Segment Your List**: Use segmentation to tailor your email content to different audience groups based on their interests and behaviors.

Example: Amazon sends personalized product recommendations based on users' past purchases and browsing history.

Paid Promotion Basics

Paid promotion involves using advertising options to reach a broader audience and drive traffic to your content.

1. Introduction to Paid Advertising

Paid advertising can accelerate your content's visibility and reach, offering various options to target specific audiences.

Steps to Utilize Paid Advertising:

- ❖ **Choose the Right Platforms**: Select advertising platforms that align with your audience and goals. Common options include Google Ads, Facebook Ads, and LinkedIn Ads.

Example: Shopify uses Google Ads and Facebook Ads to target potential customers searching for e-commerce solutions and online business tools.

- ❖ **Set Clear Objectives**: Define your advertising goals, such as increasing traffic, generating leads, or boosting sales.

Example: Airbnb's ad campaigns often focus on driving bookings and increasing brand awareness among travelers.

- ❖ **Create Targeted Ads**: Develop ad creatives and copy that resonate with your target audience and align with your objectives.

Example: Grammarly's ads highlight the tool's key benefits and use compelling visuals to attract users looking for writing improvement.

2. Budgeting and Bidding

Effective budgeting and bidding strategies are essential for optimizing your ad spend and achieving desired results.

Steps for Budgeting and Bidding:

- ❖ **Set a Budget**: Determine how much you're willing to spend on paid advertising and allocate your budget accordingly.

Example: Spotify's ad campaigns often involve setting clear budgets and adjusting bids based on performance and goals.

- ❖ **Choose Bidding Strategies**: Select bidding strategies that align with your goals, such as cost-per-click (CPC) or cost-per-impression (CPM).

Example: Google Ads offers various bidding strategies, including manual CPC and automated bidding options, to optimize ad performance.

- ❖ **Monitor and Adjust**: Regularly review ad performance and make adjustments to optimize your campaigns and maximize ROI.

Example: Facebook Ads Manager provides detailed performance metrics that allow advertisers to refine their strategies and improve results.

Building Partnerships

Collaborating with influencers and other creators can extend your reach and enhance your content's credibility.

1. Collaborating with Influencers

Influencers can help promote your content to their established audiences, driving traffic and engagement.

Steps to Collaborate with Influencers:

- ❖ **Identify Relevant Influencers**: Find influencers whose audience aligns with your target demographic and whose values align with your brand.

Example: Daniel Wellington partnered with Instagram influencers to promote their watches, leveraging their followers to increase brand visibility.

- ❖ **Build Relationships**: Establish genuine relationships with influencers by engaging with their content and offering value in return.

Example: Glossier has successfully built relationships with beauty influencers, resulting in authentic endorsements and increased brand awareness.

- ❖ **Create Collaborative Content**: Work with influencers to create content that showcases your brand in an authentic and engaging manner.

Example: Red Bull's collaborations with extreme sports athletes produce compelling content that aligns with their brand's adventurous spirit.

2. Partnering with Other Creators

Collaborating with other content creators can help you reach new audiences and add value to your content.

Steps to Partner with Creators:

- **Find Complementary Creators**: Identify creators whose content complements yours and who share a similar target audience.

Example: The collaboration between Marie Forleo and Tony Robbins combined their expertise to create valuable content for their respective audiences.

- **Plan Collaborative Projects**: Develop joint projects, such as co-authored content, webinars, or live events, that provide value to both audiences.

Example: The creators of "The Minimalists" podcast collaborated with other minimalism advocates to create a comprehensive online course.

- **Cross-Promote Content**: Use each other's platforms to promote the collaborative content and drive traffic to both parties' channels.

Example: The collaboration between NPR and the creators of "Serial" podcast helped drive traffic and increase listenership for both parties.

Your audience isn't found; it's understood. The more you know them, the louder your message will resonate.

Chapter Nine

Measuring and Analyzing Success

Measuring and analyzing the success of your content is crucial for understanding its impact and making informed decisions for future improvements. This chapter explores how to track key metrics, analyze data effectively, and refine your approach based on insights and feedback.

Tracking Key Metrics

To gauge the effectiveness of your content, you need to identify and monitor key performance indicators (KPIs) that align with your goals. These metrics provide insight into how well your content is performing and where adjustments might be needed.

1. Defining Your KPIs

KPIs should reflect your content goals and help you measure success.

Steps to Define Your KPIs:

- ❖ **Set Clear Goals**: Determine what you want to achieve with your content, such as increasing traffic, generating leads, or boosting engagement.

Example: If your goal is to increase brand awareness, KPIs might include metrics like reach, impressions, and social media mentions.

- ❖ **Choose Relevant Metrics**: Select metrics that align with your goals. Common KPIs include:
  - ➤ **Traffic Metrics**: Page views, unique visitors, and referral sources.
  - ➤ **Engagement Metrics**: Likes, shares, comments, and average time on page.
  - ➤ **Conversion Metrics**: Click-through rates (CTR), conversion rates, and lead generation.

Example: HubSpot tracks metrics such as blog views, email open rates, and conversion rates to measure the effectiveness of their content marketing efforts.

2. Using Analytics Tools

Analytics tools help you track and measure these metrics effectively.

Steps to Use Analytics Tools:

- **Implement Google Analytics**: Set up Google Analytics to monitor website traffic, user behavior, and conversion data.

Example: Google Analytics provides insights into user demographics, behavior flow, and traffic sources, helping you understand how users interact with your content.

- **Use Social Media Insights**: Leverage the analytics tools provided by social media platforms to track engagement, reach, and audience growth.

Example: Facebook Insights and Twitter Analytics offer detailed reports on post-performance, audience demographics, and engagement levels.

- **Monitor Email Performance**: Track metrics like open rates, click rates, and unsubscribe rates to assess the effectiveness of your email campaigns.

Example: Mailchimp provides detailed reports on email campaign performance, including subscriber engagement and conversion rates.

Analyzing Data

Once you've collected data, the next step is to analyze it to gain valuable insights and assess your content strategy's effectiveness.

1. Interpreting Metrics

Understanding what your metrics are telling you is key to making data-driven decisions.

Steps to Interpret Metrics:

- ❖ **Identify Trends**: Look for patterns in your data, such as increases in traffic during specific times or high engagement on certain content types.

Example: If you notice that blog posts with visual content receive more shares, it may indicate a preference for visual media among your audience.

- ❖ **Compare Performance**: Compare current data with historical data or benchmarks to assess improvements or declines in performance.

Example: Compare this month's traffic to last months to evaluate whether recent changes in your content strategy are having a positive impact.

- **Assess Content Effectiveness**: Determine which content pieces are performing well and which are not meeting expectations.

Example: Analyze which blog posts generate the most leads and replicate their successful elements in future content.

2. Using Insights for Improvement

Use the insights gained from your data analysis to refine and enhance your content strategy.

Steps to Use Insights for Improvement:

- **Identify Strengths and Weaknesses**: Determine what's working well and what needs improvement based on your data.

Example: If certain topics or formats consistently perform better, consider focusing more on those areas.

- **Adjust Content Strategy**: Modify your content strategy based on your findings, such as creating more content on popular topics or improving areas where performance is lacking.

Example: If you find that blog posts with how-to guides receive higher engagement, consider increasing the frequency of such content.

- ❖ **Experiment and Test**: Conduct A/B tests or experiments to test new ideas and strategies, and measure their impact on performance.

Example: Test different headlines or formats for your email campaigns to see which results in higher open or click-through rates.

Refining Your Approach

Refining your approach based on feedback and performance data ensures continuous improvement and aligns your content strategy with your audience's needs and preferences.

1. Gathering Feedback

Collecting feedback from your audience and stakeholders provides additional insights into your content's effectiveness.

Steps to Gather Feedback:

- **Conduct Surveys**: Use surveys to gather opinions from your audience about what they like and what they want more of.

Example: Send out a survey to your email list asking for feedback on recent content and suggestions for future topics.

- **Monitor Social Media Conversations**: Pay attention to comments and discussions on social media to understand how your audience is responding to your content.

Example: Analyze social media comments to gauge audience sentiment and identify common questions or concerns.

- **Solicit Direct Feedback**: Engage with your audience through comments, emails, or direct messages to gather feedback on specific pieces of content.

Example: Ask readers for their thoughts on a recent blog post or video and use their input to inform future content.

2. Making Data-Driven Decisions

Use the combined insights from data analysis and feedback to make informed decisions about your content strategy.

Steps for Data-Driven Decision-Making:

- ❖ **Prioritize Changes**: Focus on implementing changes that will have the most significant impact based on your analysis and feedback.

Example: If your data shows that mobile users are experiencing issues, prioritize optimizing your content for mobile devices.

- ❖ **Set New Goals**: Based on your insights, set new goals and KPIs to drive future content efforts and measure progress.

Example: If you've achieved your initial traffic goals, set new goals for increasing engagement or generating leads.

- ❖ **Continuously Monitor and Adjust**: Regularly review your metrics and feedback to ensure your content strategy remains effective and relevant.

Chapter Ten

Establishing Consistency and Reliability

Consistency and reliability are the cornerstones of building a successful content empire. They ensure that your audience knows what to expect and continues to engage with your brand over time. This chapter covers how to establish robust content creation routines, maintain high-quality standards, and foster ongoing interaction with your audience.

Content Creation Routines

Developing habits and systems for consistent content output is essential for maintaining audience engagement and establishing your brand's reliability.

1. Creating a Content Calendar

A content calendar helps you plan, organize, and schedule your content in advance, ensuring that you consistently deliver valuable material to your audience.

Steps to Create a Content Calendar:

- **Identify Key Dates and Themes**: Plan content around important dates, industry events, or seasonal themes relevant to your audience.

Example: If you run a fitness blog, schedule content around New Year's resolutions, summer fitness tips, or holiday fitness challenges.

- **Plan Content Types and Formats**: Diversify your content by including blog posts, videos, infographics, and social media updates in your calendar.

Example: Include weekly blog posts, monthly videos, and daily social media updates to keep your content varied and engaging.

- **Set Deadlines and Assign Tasks**: Establish deadlines for content creation and assign tasks to team members or collaborators to ensure timely delivery.

Example: Assign blog post drafts to writers, graphic design tasks to designers, and social media promotion tasks to your marketing team.

2. Developing Content Creation Habits

Establishing consistent habits can help streamline the content creation process and ensure regular output.

Steps to Develop Content Creation Habits:

- ❖ **Set Aside Dedicated Time**: Allocate specific times in your schedule for content creation, editing, and planning.

Example: Dedicate Monday mornings to brainstorming and planning, Tuesday and Wednesday afternoons to writing, and Thursday to editing and finalizing content.

- ❖ **Create a Content Creation Workflow**: Develop a step-by-step process for creating, reviewing, and publishing content.

Example: Your workflow might include brainstorming, drafting, reviewing, editing, and publishing, with specific checklists for each stage.

- ❖ **Use Tools and Templates**: Utilize tools and templates to streamline content creation and maintain consistency in format and style.

Example: Use content templates for blog posts, social media graphics, and email newsletters to ensure a cohesive look and feel.

Maintaining Quality Over Time

As your content empire grows, maintaining high-quality standards becomes increasingly important to retain your audience's trust and engagement.

1. Implementing Quality Control Measures

Quality control measures help ensure that your content meets high standards before publication.

Steps to Implement Quality Control:

- ❖ **Establish Content Guidelines**: Create detailed guidelines covering tone, style, formatting, and accuracy to ensure consistency across all content.

Example: Develop a style guide for your blog that outlines preferred writing styles, formatting rules, and editorial standards.

- ❖ **Conduct Regular Reviews**: Implement a review process where content is checked for accuracy, clarity, and alignment with your brand's standards.

Example: Have a dedicated editor review all content before publication to catch errors and ensure it meets quality standards.

- ❖ **Gather Feedback and Iterate**: Collect feedback from your audience and team members to identify areas for improvement and make necessary adjustments.

Example: Use surveys or feedback forms to gather input on content quality and incorporate suggestions for future content.

2. Investing in Professional Development

Continuous learning and professional development can help you and your team stay updated with industry trends and improve content quality.

Steps for Professional Development:

- ❖ **Attend Workshops and Conferences**: Participate in industry events to learn new techniques and stay informed about emerging trends.

Example: Attend content marketing conferences to gain insights into the latest strategies and tools for improving content quality.

- ❖ **Pursue Online Courses and Certifications**: Enroll in online courses or obtain certifications to enhance your skills and knowledge in content creation and marketing.

Example: Take courses on platforms like Coursera or LinkedIn Learning to improve your writing, SEO, or graphic design skills.

- ❖ **Encourage Continuous Learning**: Foster a culture of continuous learning within your team by sharing resources and encouraging skill development.

Example: Set up a team learning library or provide access to industry publications and training resources.

Engaging with Your Audience

Ongoing interaction and community building are crucial for maintaining audience loyalty and fostering a sense of connection with your brand.

1. Building a community

Creating a sense of community helps your audience feel more connected to your brand and encourages ongoing engagement.

Steps to Build a community:

- **Create Interactive Content**: Develop content that encourages participation, such as polls, quizzes, and discussion prompts.

Example: Run a weekly Q&A session or create interactive quizzes related to your content topics to engage your audience.

- **Host Live Events and Webinars**: Organize live events or webinars to interact with your audience in real time and provide valuable insights.

Example: Host a live webinar on a relevant topic and invite your audience to ask questions and participate in the discussion.

- **Foster Engagement through social media**: Use social media platforms to connect with your audience, respond to comments, and participate in conversations.

Example: Regularly engage with followers on social media by responding to comments, sharing user-generated content, and participating in relevant discussions.

2. Encouraging User-Generated Content

User-generated content (UGC) can enhance engagement and build a stronger connection with your audience.

Steps to Encourage UGC:

- **Create Contests and Challenges**: Run contests or challenges that encourage your audience to create and share content related to your brand.

Example: Launch a photo contest where users submit images related to your brand's theme, and feature the best submissions on your website or social media.

- **Feature User Contributions**: Showcase user-generated content on your platforms to highlight and reward active community members.

Example: Create a "Community Spotlight" section on your blog or social media profiles to feature content submitted by your audience.

- **Acknowledge and Appreciate**: Show appreciation for your audience's contributions by thanking them publicly and acknowledging their support.

Example: Send personalized thank-you messages or offer exclusive rewards to users who regularly contribute valuable content or feedback.

Establishing consistency and reliability involves developing content creation routines, maintaining high-quality standards, and actively engaging with your audience. By creating effective habits, ensuring quality, and fostering community interaction, you can build a strong and reliable content empire that resonates with your audience and stands the test of time.

Authenticity is the currency of trust in the digital age, invest in it wisely, and your brand will never go bankrupt

Chapter Eleven

Scaling Your Efforts

As your content empire grows, scaling your efforts becomes crucial to managing increased demand and maximizing your impact. This chapter explores effective strategies for outsourcing and delegation, leveraging tools and technology, and expanding your reach to grow your audience and enhance your content's influence.

Outsourcing and Delegation

Building a capable team or collaborating with freelancers can help manage the growing demands of content creation and ensure that your brand maintains high standards.

1. Identifying Key Roles and Responsibilities

Determine which aspects of content creation and management can be outsourced or delegated to optimize efficiency and focus on strategic tasks.

Steps to Identify Key Roles:

- ❖ **Assess Your Needs**: Evaluate your current content operations and identify areas where additional support is needed.

Example: If your content production is expanding, you might need additional writers, designers, or social media managers.

- ❖ **Define Roles and Responsibilities**: Clearly outline the roles and responsibilities for each position or freelance contractor.

Example: Create job descriptions for content writers, graphic designers, and social media specialists detailing their specific tasks and expectations.

- ❖ **Determine Skill Requirements**: Identify the skills and expertise required for each role to ensure you hire or collaborate with qualified individuals.

Example: For a content strategist role, seek candidates with experience in content planning, SEO, and analytics.

2. Finding and Managing Freelancers

Freelancers can provide specialized skills and flexibility to scale your content efforts effectively.

Steps to Find and Manage Freelancers:

- ❖ **Use Freelance Platforms**: Explore platforms like Upwork, Fiverr, and Freelancer to find skilled freelancers for various tasks.

Example: Hire a freelance graphic designer to create high-quality visuals or a content writer to produce blog posts.

- **Evaluate Portfolios and References**: Review freelancers' portfolios and seek references to assess their expertise and reliability.

Example: Check past work samples and client reviews to ensure the freelancer's style and quality align with your brand's standards.

- **Establish Clear Communication**: Set up clear communication channels and guidelines to ensure smooth collaboration and project management.

Example: Use project management tools like Asana or Trello to track tasks and deadlines, and maintain regular check-ins with freelancers.

3. Building an Internal Team

As your content empire grows, building an internal team may be necessary for more long-term and integrated support.

Steps to Build an Internal Team:

- ❖ **Recruit Talented Individuals**: Hire full-time or part-time staff to handle critical functions such as content creation, strategy, and marketing.

Example: Recruit a content manager to oversee the content calendar and ensure quality control, or a social media manager to handle engagement and promotion.

- ❖ **Foster a Collaborative Culture**: Create a positive work environment that encourages collaboration and innovation within your team.

Example: Organize regular team meetings and brainstorming sessions to discuss new ideas and strategies.

- ❖ **Provide Training and Development**: Invest in training and professional development to enhance your team's skills and keep them updated with industry trends.

Example: Offer workshops or online courses on the latest content marketing techniques or tools.

Utilizing Tools and Technology

Leveraging the right tools and technology can streamline your content management processes, enhance efficiency, and provide valuable insights.

1. Content Management Systems (CMS)

A robust CMS helps you manage, organize, and publish content efficiently.

Steps to Choose and Use a CMS:

- ❖ **Evaluate Your Needs**: Assess your content management requirements and choose a CMS that fits your needs.

Example: WordPress is a popular CMS for its flexibility and extensive plugin ecosystem, while HubSpot offers integrated content management and marketing features.

- ❖ **Utilize CMS Features**: Take advantage of CMS features such as content scheduling, user management, and SEO optimization tools.

Example: Use WordPress's scheduling feature to plan and automate content publishing, and its SEO plugins to optimize content for search engines.

- **Integrate with Other Tools**: Integrate your CMS with other tools such as email marketing platforms, social media schedulers, and analytics tools for seamless management.

Example: Connect your CMS with Mailchimp for automated email campaigns or Hootsuite for social media scheduling.

2. Analytics and Reporting Tools

Analytics tools provide insights into content performance and audience behavior.

Steps to Utilize Analytics Tools:

- **Implement Tracking Tools**: Use tools like Google Analytics, SEMrush, or Ahrefs to track website traffic, user behavior, and SEO performance.

Example: Google Analytics provides detailed reports on traffic sources, user demographics, and behavior flow, helping you understand how users interact with your content.

- **Monitor Key Metrics**: Regularly review key performance indicators (KPIs) to assess the effectiveness of your content strategy.

Example: Track metrics such as page views, bounce rates, and conversion rates to evaluate content performance.

- ❖ **Generate Reports**: Create and analyze reports to gain insights into trends and make data-driven decisions.

Example: Generate monthly reports to review content performance and adjust your strategy based on the findings.

3. Content Creation and Collaboration Tools

Utilize tools that enhance content creation and streamline collaboration among team members.

Steps to Use Content Creation Tools:

- ❖ **Explore Design and Editing Tools**: Use tools like Canva, Adobe Creative Suite, or Grammarly to create and edit high-quality content.

Example: Canva offers user-friendly templates and design tools for creating visually appealing graphics and social media posts.

- ❖ **Implement Collaboration Platforms**: Utilize collaboration tools such as Slack or Microsoft Teams to facilitate communication and project management among team members.

Example: Use Slack for real-time messaging and file sharing, and Asana for task management and project tracking.

- ❖ **Adopt Automation Tools**: Leverage automation tools to streamline repetitive tasks such as social media posting and email marketing.

Example: Use Buffer or Hootsuite to automate social media scheduling and Mailchimp for automated email campaigns.

Expanding Your Reach

To grow your audience and increase your content's impact, implement strategies that broaden your reach and enhance visibility.

1. Leveraging SEO and SEM

Search engine optimization (SEO) and search engine marketing (SEM) can drive organic and paid traffic to your content.

Steps for SEO and SEM:

- ❖ **Optimize for SEO**: Ensure your content is optimized for relevant keywords, includes meta tags, and adheres to SEO best practices.

Example: Conduct keyword research and incorporate high-ranking keywords into your content, titles, and meta descriptions to improve search engine visibility.

- ❖ **Utilize SEM Campaigns**: Invest in paid search advertising to target specific keywords and drive traffic to your content.

Example: Run Google Ads campaigns targeting keywords related to your content to attract visitors interested in your niche.

- ❖ **Monitor and Adjust**: Continuously monitor your SEO and SEM performance and make adjustments based on data and trends.

Example: Use tools like Google Search Console to track search performance and adjust your SEO strategy accordingly.

2. Expanding to New Platforms

Explore new platforms and channels to reach a broader audience and diversify your content distribution.

Steps to Expand to New Platforms:

- **Identify New Channels**: Research and identify platforms where your target audience is active, such as emerging social media networks or niche forums.

Example: If you're in the tech industry, consider expanding to platforms like Reddit's tech communities or specialized tech forums.

- **Adapt Content for Each Platform**: Tailor your content to fit the format and audience of each new platform.

Example: Create short, engaging videos for TikTok or LinkedIn articles for a professional audience.

- **Engage with Platform Communities**: Actively participate in discussions and engage with users on new platforms to build relationships and increase visibility.

Example: Join relevant groups or forums and contribute valuable insights to establish your presence and attract followers.

3. Building Strategic Partnerships

Forming partnerships with other brands or influencers can enhance your reach and credibility.

Steps for Building Partnerships:

- **Identify Potential Partners**: Look for brands or influencers with complementary audiences and shared values.

Example: Partner with industry influencers for guest posts, joint webinars, or collaborative content to tap into their follower base.

- **Develop Collaborative Projects**: Work on projects such as co-branded content, joint events, or cross-promotions to expand your reach.

Example: Collaborate with an influencer to create a series of co-branded blog posts or videos that benefit both parties.

- **Measure Partnership Impact**: Track the performance of your partnerships and assess their effectiveness in reaching new audiences and achieving content goals.

Example: Monitor metrics such as referral traffic, engagement rates, and conversion rates from partnership campaigns.

Scaling your content efforts involves outsourcing and delegation, utilizing essential tools and technology, and implementing strategies to expand your reach. By building a capable team, leveraging advanced tools, and exploring new platforms and partnerships, you can effectively grow your content empire and enhance its impact.

Chapter Twelve:
Setting the Stage for Future Phases

As you establish your content empire, it's crucial to lay the groundwork for future growth and success. This chapter focuses on long-term planning, building a strong foundation, and preparing for the transition to advanced strategies and scaling techniques in subsequent phases.

Long-Term Planning

Effective long-term planning is essential for scaling your content empire and preparing for monetization. This phase involves envisioning where you want your content brand to go and how you will achieve those goals.

1. Defining Your Vision for Growth

A clear vision helps guide your strategic decisions and ensures that your content empire evolves in a way that aligns with your long-term goals.

Steps to Define Your Vision:

- ❖ **Set Ambitious Goals**: Establish specific, measurable, achievable, relevant, and time-bound (SMART) goals for growth and monetization.

Example: Aim to increase your audience size by 50% in the next year or achieve a certain revenue milestone through content monetization strategies.

- ❖ **Identify Key Milestones**: Outline key milestones and achievements that will mark progress towards your long-term goals.

Example: Milestones might include launching new content formats, securing partnerships, or reaching specific revenue targets.

- ❖ **Develop a Strategic Roadmap**: Create a roadmap that details the steps and strategies needed to reach your long-term goals.

Example: Your roadmap could include phases such as expanding content offerings, exploring new revenue streams, and enhancing audience engagement.

2. Exploring Monetization Opportunities

Monetizing your content empire requires careful planning and consideration of various revenue streams.

Steps to Explore Monetization:

- ❖ **Evaluate Revenue Streams**: Research and assess potential revenue streams such as advertising, sponsored content, affiliate marketing, or subscription models.

Example: Consider integrating sponsored posts into your content strategy or launching a premium membership program for exclusive content.

- ❖ **Develop a Monetization Strategy**: Create a strategy that outlines how you will implement and manage your chosen revenue streams.

Example: Develop a plan for approaching potential sponsors, setting pricing models for advertising, and promoting your subscription services.

- ❖ **Test and Refine**: Start with pilot projects or small-scale tests to evaluate the effectiveness of different monetization strategies and refine your approach based on results.

Example: Test sponsored content with a few brands and assess performance before scaling up to larger partnerships.

Building a Strong Foundation

A solid foundation ensures that your current efforts support sustainable growth and long-term success.

1. Strengthening Your Brand

A strong brand foundation enhances your content's credibility and appeal, supporting future growth.

Steps to Strengthen Your Brand:

- ❖ **Enhance Your Brand Identity**: Continuously refine your brand's voice, tone, and visual identity to ensure consistency and relevance.

Example: Regularly review and update your brand guidelines to reflect any changes in your brand's positioning or audience preferences.

- ❖ **Build Brand Loyalty**: Foster strong relationships with your audience through consistent engagement and delivering value.

Example: Implement loyalty programs or exclusive content for your most dedicated followers to reinforce brand loyalty.

- **Maintain High Quality**: Ensure that all content meets high standards of quality to build trust and retain your audience.

Example: Regularly review and update your quality control processes to keep pace with evolving industry standards and audience expectations.

2. Strengthening Your Operations

Efficient operations support sustainable growth and help manage increased demands as your content empire expands.

Steps to Strengthen Operations:

- **Optimize Workflows**: Streamline content creation, approval, and distribution processes to enhance efficiency.

Example: Use project management tools to track tasks and deadlines, and automate routine tasks where possible.

- **Invest in Infrastructure**: Upgrade your technical infrastructure to support increased content volume and audience engagement.

Example: Invest in scalable hosting solutions and content delivery networks (CDNs) to ensure fast and reliable content delivery.

- ❖ **Build a Strong Team**: Develop a skilled and motivated team capable of supporting your growth and adapting to changing needs.

Example: Provide ongoing training and professional development to keep your team's skills current and aligned with industry trends.

In the Next book

Transitioning to advanced strategies and scaling techniques involves building on the foundation you've established and preparing for the next phase of growth.

1. Preparing for Advanced Strategies

Plan and prepare for advanced strategies that will help you scale your content empire further.

Steps to Prepare:

- ❖ **Research Advanced Techniques**: Explore advanced content marketing strategies, emerging trends, and innovative approaches that can drive growth.

Example: Investigate trends such as AI-driven content personalization or advanced analytics techniques to stay ahead of the curve.

- **Pilot New Initiatives**: Test new strategies on a smaller scale to evaluate their potential impact and effectiveness.

Example: Launch a pilot program for a new content format or distribution channel to assess audience response before full-scale implementation.

- **Evaluate Resource Needs**: Assess additional resources or investments required to implement advanced strategies.

Example: Determine if you need to invest in new technology, hire additional team members, or allocate a larger budget for marketing initiatives.

2. Planning for Scaling

Develop a detailed plan for scaling your content empire to accommodate increased audience size and content volume.

Steps to Plan for Scaling:

- **Create a Scaling Strategy**: Outline a strategy for scaling your content operations, including hiring, technology, and process improvements.

Example: Develop a plan for expanding your team, upgrading your CMS, and optimizing content production workflows to handle increased demands.

- **Implement Scalable Systems**: Invest in systems and processes that can grow with your content empire.

Example: Use scalable cloud-based solutions for content management and distribution to handle increased traffic and content volume.

- **Monitor and Adjust**: Continuously monitor your scaling efforts and make adjustments based on performance and feedback.

Setting the stage for future phases involves long-term planning, building a strong foundation, and preparing for advanced strategies. By defining your vision for growth, strengthening your brand and operations, and planning for scaling, you can ensure that your content empire is well-positioned for continued success and impact.

www.ingramcontent.com/pod-product-compliance
Lightning Source LLC
Chambersburg PA
CBHW050312230526
45471CB00005B/2136